Diners

American Retro

Unanimous

Diners

American Retro

Take outs are fine,

but please leave

the tables and chairs.

'50s diner logo

Contents

Introduction

"On that road the nation is steadily traveling beyond the troubles of this century, constantly heading toward finer tomorrows. The American Road is paved with hope."

1951 Ford ad

The great highways of America were its very heart and soul. They spanned the limits of this vast country from top to bottom and east to west. They carried the new breed of motorists from good to bad, from boom to bust, through towns with such names as Mammoth Cave, Kentucky; Pleasantville, New York; and Broken Bow, Nebraska; many of them with nothing more than a Main Street and a drugstore.

Along the way these arteries offered succor in the form of welcoming diners, serving plates of wholesome freshly prepared dishes—food that spawned a universal language in the shape of hot dogs, hamburgers, fries, and malts. Comfortable motels with warm rooms offered the latest in modern conveniences, from power showers to the combination television and radio set, and provided a safe haven for the night. They were clean and affordable family businesses, which allowed the nuclear family, for the first time, to explore the wonders of their own land.

Parked outside were the trappings of prosperity—Cadillacs, T-Birds, Chevrolets, and Corvettes—cars that any sane person has always wanted to drive. These were elongated giants, explosions of chrome grilles and wire wheels, creating fantasies of speed and escapism with features taken from aircraft designs and space travel. These were the only beasts capable of taming this extraordinary country, and are as representative of the United States of America as the Statue of Liberty or the Stars and Stripes.

The names of those great roads—Highway 61, Route 66, Pacific 1—have since passed into popular mythology. For those with a passion for adventure, the names evoke images of *Easy Rider*, and the lyrics of Bob Dylan and the Rolling Stones. At the same time, they are able to convey that air of safety and innocence, when mom and pop ushered the kids into the back of the family automobile and headed off on vacation.

Now this golden age is all but gone, although remnants do remain. The highways have fallen into disrepair, superseded by freeways with no recognizable character. Many diners have served their last "special," and a large number of "ma and pa" motels have been swallowed up into chains with such alluring names as Comfort Inn and Motel 6 (we are never told what happened to Motels 1 through 5). Small towns, with the whole of life encapsulated on Main Street, are a far cry from the soulless shopping malls of today. And the cars—oh those glorious, gas-guzzling monsters—have been replaced by sensible, compact, economical models with dull names.

As a tribute to the post-war period when people had money in their pockets and a hankering to spend it, the four titles in the *American Retro* series draw on images, both retro and modern, that resonate with the spirit of '50s America. These pictures are paired with advertising slogans, popular sayings, puns, and quotations from personalities that bring to life an age when being economical with the truth came naturally to the advertisers and salesmen of the day, who were desperate to paint a dazzling and futuristic world in which everyone could share. Motels shamelessly claimed to offer comfort fit for the "Queen of Sheba"; car manufacturers used such buzz words as "Rocket Ride" and "Glamorous new Futuramics"; and diners bedecked themselves in chrome detailing and neon lights.

The *American Retro* series recaptures a little of what made those times so special, with images that will fill those who lived through that age with nostalgia and gently amuse and inform those who did not. Read, remember, and enjoy.

I don't know what your destiny will be, but one thing I do know: the only ones among you who will be really happy are those who have sought and found how to serve.

Albert Schweitzer

Clean as a whistle.

'50s diner logo

How do you like your eggs?

$3

HAM STEAK &

Las Vegas, Nevada

Lanai CAFE

STEAK & EGGS
$2.99

.95

EGGS

San Francisco, California

Marion, Virginia17

Never eat more

than you can lift.

Miss Piggy

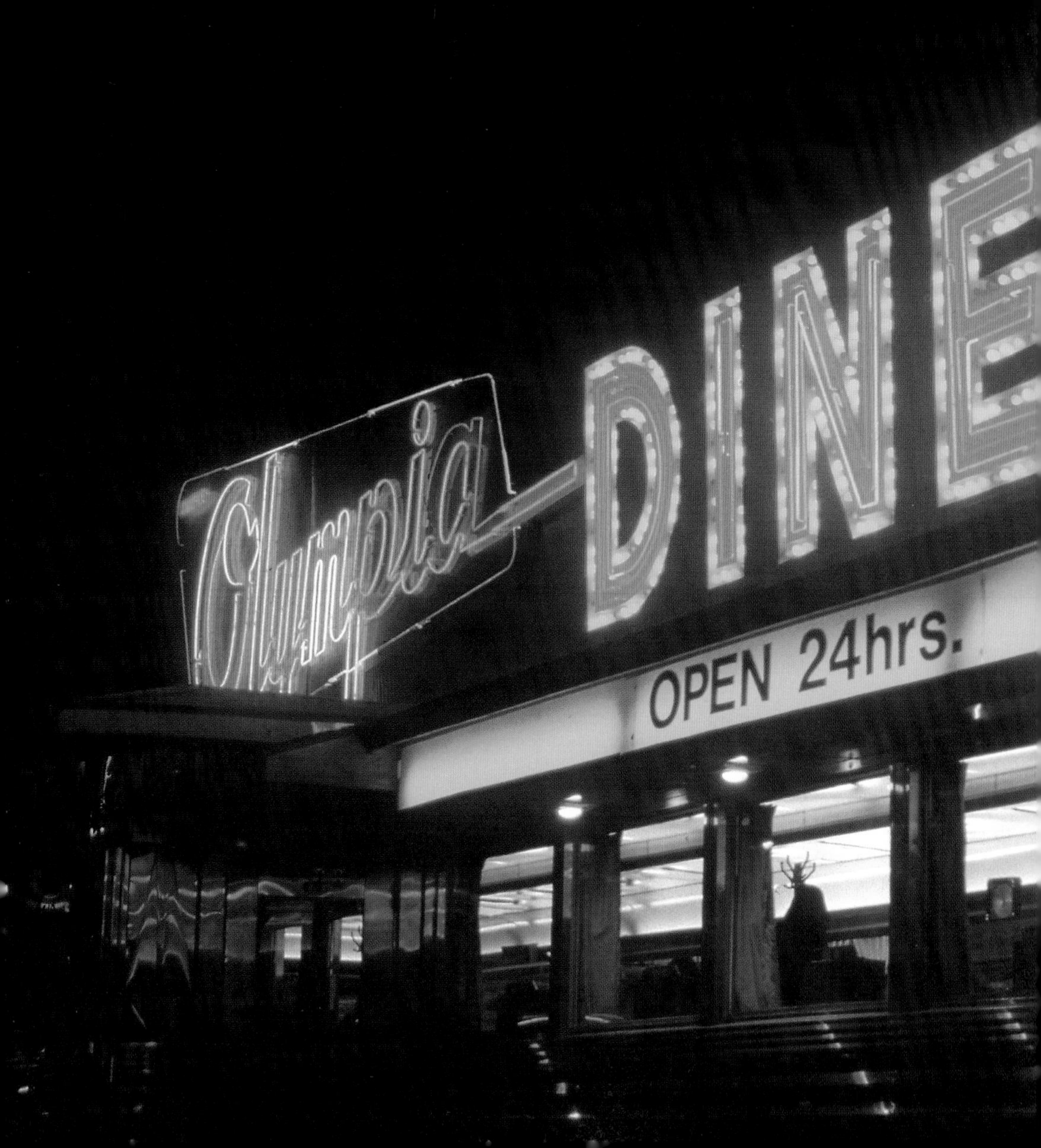
Olympia
DINE
OPEN 24hrs.

Without an architecture of
our own we have no soul of
our own civilization.

Frank Lloyd Wright

Good and wholesome always.

'50s diner logo

Ever notice that

"What the hell"

is always the right decision?

Marilyn Monroe

Can't spell; can cook.

Shamrock, Texas

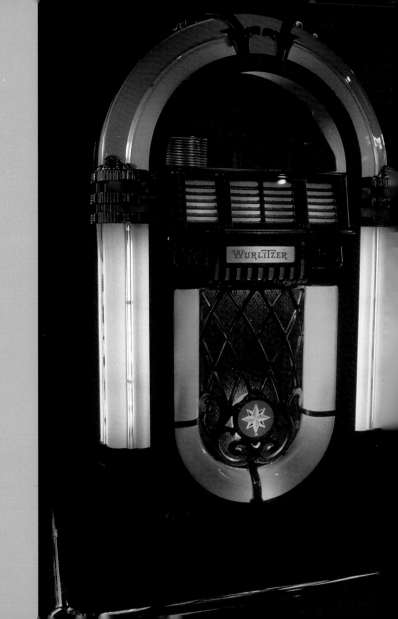

Stay tuned for more rock and roll.

Cup of Joe to go.

'50s diner logo

New York City

Lexington Hiball.

'50s diner glassware logo

Postcard from the Hub
Diner, Beaumont, Texas

For food that's

out of this world.

Take outs are fine, but please leave the tables and chairs.

'50s diner logo

Front Royal, Virginia

We'll take our regular booth.

Like grandma's, only more so.

Every great architect is—necessarily—a great poet. He must be a great original interpreter of his time, his day, his age.

Frank Lloyd Wright

Warrenton, Virginia

Form never follows function.

Diner shaped like a
dirigible airship in Los Angeles

The whole of society

can be found in a small town diner.

Pittsburgh, New Hampshire

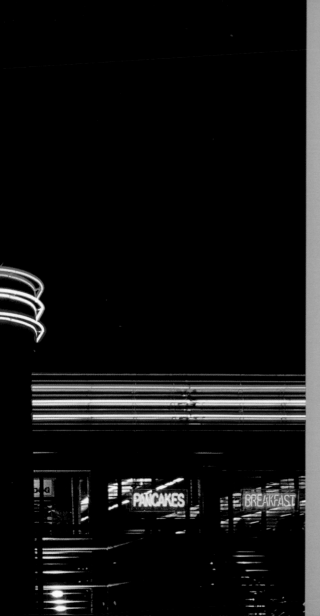

All architecture is great
architecture after sunset;

perhaps architecture is really
a nocturnal art,
like the art of fireworks.

G. K. Chesterton

You can tell the ideals

of a nation by its advertising.

New York City

I am not a glutton—

I am an explorer of food.

Erma Louise Bombeck

TIME TO EAT

Loris

DINER

OPEN
24
HOURS

OPEN

Loris
DINER

Pass the ketchup.

Johnny Rockets hits the spot.

'50s diner logo

Los Angeles, California

No dancin' in the aisles.

'50s diner logo

Ich bin ein Frankfurter.

San Francisco, California

The national dish of America is menus.

Robert Robinson

Los Angeles, California

SPECIALS

COFFEE CAKES	2¢	PURE ORANGE JUICE	5¢
DOUGHNUTS	1¢	VARIETY OF SALADS	5¢
HOT BISCUITS	1¢	FRESH VEGETABLES	5¢
MUFFINS OR CORN BREAD	2¢	STEWED FRUITS	5¢
BUTTERED TOAST	1¢	LARGE PIE OR CAKE	5¢
CHICKEN OR VEG. SOUP	3¢	CHOICE OF PUDDINGS	5¢
COFFEE WITH PURE CREAM	3¢	ROAST BEEF HASH	5¢
HOT CHOCOLATE OR TEA	3¢	FISH CAKES	5¢

ALL CEREALS WITH MILK 5¢

FEWSTER'S SPECIAL DINNER

10:30 A.M. —— to —— 10 P.M.

Soup, Meat Order, Potato
and Gravy, Vegetable, Salad,
Desert, Bread & Butter
Coffee, Tea or Buttermilk

all for 20¢

Wishes won't wash dishes.

Fort Madison, Iowa

It requires a certain kind of mind to see beauty in a hamburger bun.

Ray Kroc

LY SERVICE..FAMILY PRICES
N'S DINER
LES .... EXIT 21
24 HOURS DAILY
UNITED

Open for business.

Watertown, New York

Adventure is worthwhile in itself.

As American as pecan pie.

The morning cup of coffee has an exhilaration about it

which the cheering influence of the afternoon or evening cup of tea

cannot be expected to reproduce.

Oliver Wendell Holmes, Sr.

$1.95

Breakfast

11 PM to 7 AM

Hyde Park, New York

We must stop talking about

the American dream

and start listening to

the dreams of the Americans.

Reubin Askew

Strong minded,

resolutely willed,

you can create out of

nothing a great business,

a huge empire,

a new world.

Claude M. Bristol

New York City

Drink Cheer Up.

'50s diner glassware logo

SHAVE

...enjoy your ice cream

while it's on your plate—

that's my philosophy...

Thornton Wilder

herokee Translation

ᎦᏚ $ 150	CONES, ᎣᏍᏗᎢᎢ-ᎣᎵᎣ ᏍᎵᎦᎢ		35 45 55
ᎣᎣᎢ 175	CHOCOLATE DIP CONES, ᎠᎣᏑᏚ ᎣᏍᏘᎴ ᏍᎵᎦᎢ		50 60
100	FLOATS ᎣᏫᎩᏟ ᎠᏘᎣᎢ		55 75
120	FREEZES ᎣᏁᎣᏗᏫᎠᎢ		75
120	BANANA SPLITS, ᏓᎦᎦ ᎠᎣᏘᎤ BᎢ		160
140	MALTS and SHAKES, ᎣᎣᎢ ᎠᏍ ᎣᏟᎳᏘ		75
140	SUNDAES, ᎠᎤᏪᎦ ᎠᎤᏴBᎦᎢ		60 75
160	Chocolate, Cherry, Butterscotch, Strawberry and Pineapple		
160	SUNDAES, Hot Fudge, Butter Pecan		70 85
160	**DRINKS, ᎣBᏟ ᏗᏘᎣᎢ**		
140	COKE, ROOT BEER, Dr.PEPPER, SPRITE	2	40 55 75
85	ORANGE or GRAPE SLUSH, ᏍᏟᎬᎣᏟᎣᎢ		40 55 75
70	LIMEADE or LEMONADE, ᏞᎦᎵᎵ ᏍᏟᎬᎣᏟᎣᎢ		55 75
85	ICE TEA, ᎣᎢᏟᎩ ᎠᏍᎣᎢ		40 55 75
100	COFFEE, ᎣᎦ		55
70			
70	We use "Bunny" Bread and Buns		
85			

We live in a
rainbow of chaos.

Paul Cezanne

Home is where the stomach is.

South Burlington, Vermont

The morning pick-me-up...

Picture credits

All images reproduced by permission of Corbis Images unless otherwise stated.

Page 8/9: Destin Diner in Destin, Florida; credit Dave G. Houser.

Page 10/11: Booths and stools in a diner; credit Eric Poppleton.

Page 12/13: Sign in Las Vegas, Nevada; reproduced by permission of Travel Ink/Simon Reddy.

Page 14/15: Fog City Diner in San Francisco, California; credit Morton Beebe.

Page 16/17: Neon sign points the way to a Diner in Marion, Virginia; credit Scott T. Smith.

Page 18/19: Sign for the Bun Boy restaurant in southern Indiana; credit Philip Gould.

Page 20/21: Olympia Diner near Hartford, Connecticut; credit Joseph Sohm.

Page 22/23: Waitress; credit RNT Productions.

Page 24/25: Banana split.

Page 26/27: U Drop Inn Café in Shamrock, Texas; reproduced by permission of Travel Ink/Walter Wolfe.

Page 28/29: Original jukebox in the Country Music Hall of Fame, Nashville, Tennessee; credit Philip Gould.

Page 30/31: Edge of the counter; credit David Katzenstein.

Page 32/33: Longchamps, on the corner of 42nd Street and Lexington Avenue in New York City; credit Bettmann.

Page 34/35: Postcard from the Hub Diner, Beaumont, Texas; credit Lake County Museum.

Page 36/37: Joe Btfsplk's Diner in Banff, Arizona; credit The Purcell Team.

Page 38/39: Nick's Diner in Front Royal, Virginia; credit Scott T. Smith.

Page 40/41: Two elderly farmers in a diner in Kansas; credit Philip Gould.

Page 42/43: Cherry pie; credit Carl Corey.

Page 44/45: Frost Diner in Warenton, Virginia; credit William A. Bake.

Page 46/47: Women entering the Zep Diner, shaped like a dirigible in Los Angeles, California; credit Bettmann.

Page 48/49: The Modern Diner, a historic landmark, in Pawtucket, Rhode Island, the first diner to be listed on the National Register of Historic Places; credit Bob Rowan.

Page 50/51: A policeman and a boy at Muriah's restaurant in Pittsburg, New Hampshire; credit Phil Schermeister.

Page 52/53: Destin Diner in Destin, Florida; credit Robert Holmes.

Page 54/55: Painted window in New York City; reproduced by permission of Travel Ink/Andrew Cowin.

Page 56/57: Diner at Underground Atlanta in Atlanta, Georgia; credit Nik Wheeler.

Page 58/59: Lori's Diner in San Francisco, California; credit Robert Holmes.

Page 60/61: Condiments; credit Carl Corey.

Page 62/63: Johnny Rockets in Los Angeles, California; credit Nik Wheeler.

Page 64/65: Wurlitzer jukebox at Fernandina Beach, Florida; credit Raymond Gehman.

Page 66/67: Hot Dog Café in San Francisco, California; reproduced by permission of Travel Ink/Geraint Tellem.

Page 68/69: Menu in window, Los Angeles, California; credit Bettmann.

Page 70/71: The short order cook in the Pantry Café in Fort Madison, Iowa; credit Nathan Benn.

Page 72/73: The classic American cheeseburger; credit Ron Stenzak.

Page 74/75: Billboard for Zinn's Diner near Wakarusa, Indiana; credit Bob Rowan & Progressive Images.

Page 76/77: Diner in Watertown, New York; credit John Bartholomew.

Page 78/79: Roadside diner along Route 66; reproduced by permission of Travel Ink/Walter Wolfe.

Page 80/81: Lea's Restaurant in LeCompte, Louisiana; credit Philip Gould.

Page 82/83: Landmark Diner in Atlanta, Georgia; credit Bob Krist.

Page 84/85: Sign advertising breakfast in Las Vegas, Nevada; reproduced by permission of Travel Ink/

Page 86/87: Eveready Diner in Hyde Park, New York; credit Joseph Sohm.

Page 88/89: New York City diner; credit Roger Wood.

Page 90/91: Empire Diner in New York City; credit Kevin Fleming.

Page 92/93: Diner in St Paul, Minnesota; credit Minnesota Historical Society.

Page 94/95: Teenager drinking a large milkshake in Lincoln, Nebraska; credit Genevieve Naylor.

Page 96/97: Shaved ice syrups in Minneapolis, Minnesota; credit Owen Franken.

Page 98/99: Menu in English and Cherokee in Tulsa, Oklahoma; credit Annie Griffiths Belt.

Page 100/101: Counter seating in a diner in Yountville, California; credit Robert Holmes.

Page 102/103: Pecan Pie in a diner in South Burlington, Vermont; credit Becky Luigart-Stayner.

Page 104/105: Drive-Inn in Tumcari, New Mexico; reproduced by permission Travel Ink/Walter Wolfe.

Page 106/107: Waitress serving coffee; credit Annie Griffiths Belt.

Attributions

Page 8/9: Albert Schweitzer.
Page 10/11: '50s diner logo.
Page 12/13: Anon.
Page 18/19: Miss Piggy.
Page 20/21: Frank Lloyd Wright.
Page 22/23: '50s diner logo.
Page 24/25: Marilyn Monroe.
Page 26/27: Anon.
Page 28/29: Anon.
Page 30/31: '50s diner logo.
Page 32/33: '50s diner glassware logo.
Page 36/37: Anon.
Page 38/39: '50s diner logo.
Page 40/41: Anon.
Page 42/43: Slogan of the General Food Corporation.
Page 44/45: Frank Lloyd Wright.
Page 46/47: Anon.
Page 48/49: Anon.
Page 50/51: Anon.
Page 52/53: G. K. Chesterton.

Published by Unanimous Ltd
254–258 Goswell Road, London EC1V 7RL

A CIP catalogue record for this book is
available from the British Library.

Designer: WDA
Editor: Alison Moss
Researcher: Suzie Green

1SBN: 1 903318 18 1

Printed and bound in Spain by Bookprint, S.L, Barcelona

1 2 3 4 5 6 7 8 9